What is...?

Bouncy and Stretchy

Heinemann

First published in Great Britain by Heinemann Library
an imprint of Heinemann Publishers (Oxford) Ltd
Halley Court, Jordan Hill, Oxford OX2 8EJ

MADRID ATHENS PARIS
FLORENCE PRAGUE WARSAW
PORTSMOUTH NH CHICAGO SAO PAULO
SINGAPORE TOKYO MELBOURNE AUCKLAND
IBADAN GABORONE JOHANNESBURG

© Heinemann Publishers (Oxford) Ltd

Designed by Heinemann Publishers (Oxford) Ltd
Printed in China

99 98 97 96 95
10 9 8 7 6 5 4 3 2 1

ISBN 0431 07969 2

British Library Cataloguing in Publication Data
Warbrick, Sarah
Bouncy and Stretchy. - (What is...? Series)
I. Series
500

Acknowledgements
The Publishers would like to thank the following
for the kind loan of equipment and materials used in
this book: Spoils, Bishop Stortford.
Toys supplied by Toys ЯUs Ltd,
the world's biggest toy megastore.

Special thanks to Bryan, Clare, George, Joel, Katie, Kevin,
Michael and Rose who appear in the photographs

All photography by Trevor Clifford
Commissioned photography arranged by Hilary Fletcher
Cover Photography: Trevor Clifford

Some things bounce but don't stretch.
Some things stretch but don't bounce.
Some things do both.

This book shows you what is bouncy and stretchy.

These things look different.
What differences can you see?

They are all bouncy or stretchy.

Michael blows air inside the balloon.
It stretches and grows bigger and bigger.

4

Balloons can bounce.

When this hopper toy is full of air . . .

George can sit on it and
bounce around the floor.

This key-ring uses a coil.

Look how far Joel can stretch it.

Katie is playing on her pogo stick.

The spring at the bottom of
the stick is pushed down and
then bounces back.

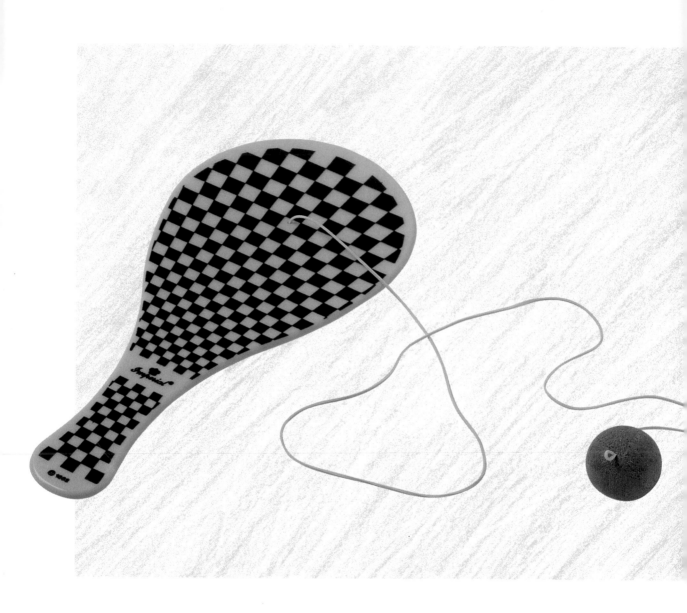

This bat and ball uses a stretchy
elastic band.

When Kevin hits the ball, the
elastic band pulls it back.

This scarf is knitted from wool.
The wool is linked together.

When the links are stretched, the
scarf grows longer.

Bryan has made a paper chain from links of different coloured strips.

He can stretch the chain so that it
reaches right across the ceiling.

This trampoline is very bouncy.
Clare can jump higher and higher.

The trampoline is elastic.
It stretches, then springs back
when she jumps up.

What is bouncy or stretchy here?

Index